Sauce Secret

A Restaurant Sauces Cookbook

SAUCE SECRETS

First edition. February 15, 2024.

Copyright © 2024 Jose Maria.

ISBN: 979-8224973705

Written by Jose Maria.

Table of Contents

Jose Maria

❖ Introduction

Welcome to the savory journey through "Sauce Secrets: A Restaurant Sauces Cookbook"! Prepare to embark on a culinary adventure where sauces reign supreme and elevate every dish to new heights of flavor and sophistication.

In the world of gastronomy, sauces are the unsung heroes that transform ordinary meals into extraordinary dining experiences. From adding depth to a simple pasta dish to complementing the richness of a perfectly grilled steak, sauces play a pivotal role in tantalizing our taste buds and satisfying our cravings.

This cookbook is a celebration of the art and craft of sauce-making, offering a comprehensive guide to mastering the techniques and flavors that define restaurant-quality cuisine. Whether you're a seasoned chef or a home cook eager to expand your culinary repertoire, you'll find inspiration and guidance within these pages.

Importance of Sauces in Elevating Dishes

Sauces are the ultimate flavor enhancers, capable of turning a mediocre meal into a memorable feast. They bring balance, complexity, and richness to dishes, elevating them from ordinary to extraordinary. A well-crafted sauce can tie together disparate elements on a plate, harmonizing flavors and textures to create a cohesive and satisfying dining experience.

Beyond their role in enhancing taste, sauces also add visual appeal to dishes, providing vibrant colors, glossy finishes, and tantalizing drizzles that entice the eye as much as the palate. They offer endless opportunities for creativity and experimentation, allowing chefs and home cooks alike to showcase their culinary prowess and signature styles.

Overview of the Cookbook's Structure and Recipes

"Sauce Secrets" is divided into eight chapters, each focusing on a different category of sauces to explore and master:

1. Essential Techniques: Learn the fundamental skills and methods for creating a wide variety of sauces, from basic stocks to complex reductions.
2. Classic French Sauces: Dive into the rich tradition of French cuisine with timeless recipes like Béchamel, Velouté, and Hollandaise, along with modern twists and pairing suggestions.
3. Italian Sauces: Explore the diverse flavors of Italy with homemade pasta sauces like Marinara, Alfredo, and Pesto, as well as regional specialties and serving ideas.
4. Asian-inspired Sauces: Discover the bold and savory flavors of Asia with recipes for Soy-ginger glaze, Teriyaki, and Peanut sauce, along with fusion creations that blend Eastern and Western influences.
5. Latin American Sauces: Spice up your meals with vibrant and flavorful sauces from Latin America, including Salsa Verde, Chimichurri, and Mole, alongside authentic recipes from various countries in the region.
6. Global Fusion Sauces: Break culinary boundaries with cross-cultural blends and innovative flavor combinations inspired by international travels and culinary trends.
7. Vegan and Gluten-Free Sauces: Cater to diverse dietary preferences and restrictions with dairy-free cream sauces, plant-based gravies, and creative gluten-free alternatives.
8. Dessert Sauces and Condiments: Indulge your sweet tooth with decadent dessert sauces like Chocolate ganache and Caramel sauce, perfect for drizzling over treats or using as accompaniments.

Throughout the cookbook, you'll find step-by-step instructions, helpful tips, and tantalizing photographs to guide and inspire you on your sauce-making journey. So, grab your apron and let's get saucy!

Chapter 1: Essential Techniques

Welcome to the foundational chapter of "Sauce Secrets: A Restaurant Sauces Cookbook." Here, we delve into the fundamental techniques that form the backbone of sauce-making. Whether you're a novice cook eager to learn the basics or a seasoned chef looking to refine your skills, mastering these essential techniques will empower you to create sauces that elevate any dish to gourmet status.

1. **Basic Sauce-Making Techniques**

- Sautéing and Deglazing: Begin by sautéing aromatics such as onions, garlic, and herbs in a bit of fat (like butter or oil) until fragrant and translucent. Deglaze the pan with a flavorful liquid, such as wine or broth, to loosen any browned bits and infuse the sauce with depth of flavor.
- Whisking and Stirring: Whisking is crucial for incorporating ingredients smoothly and evenly, preventing lumps and ensuring a velvety texture. Stirring helps to prevent scorching and encourages even cooking throughout the sauce.
- Simmering and Reduction: Simmering gently cooks the sauce, allowing flavors to meld and intensify. Reduction involves simmering the sauce uncovered to evaporate excess liquid, concentrating flavors and achieving desired thickness.

1. **Thickening Agents and Their Uses**

- Roux: A roux is a mixture of equal parts fat and flour, cooked together until golden brown. It serves as a base for many classic sauces, providing both flavor and thickening power.
- Slurry: A slurry is a mixture of starch (such as cornstarch or arrowroot) and cold liquid (such as water or broth), added to

a simmering sauce to thicken it. Unlike roux, which must be cooked to eliminate the raw flour taste, a slurry thickens instantly and is ideal for last-minute adjustments.

- Reduction: Allowing a sauce to simmer and reduce naturally thickens it as excess moisture evaporates. This method intensifies flavors while achieving the desired consistency.

1. **Emulsification and Reduction Methods**

- Emulsification: Emulsification is the process of combining two liquids that don't naturally mix, such as oil and vinegar, into a smooth, stable mixture. Common emulsified sauces include vinaigrettes and mayonnaise, achieved by slowly drizzling one ingredient into the other while whisking vigorously.
- Reduction: Reduction involves simmering a sauce to evaporate excess liquid, concentrating flavors and thickening the mixture. This method is particularly effective for creating rich, intense sauces with a velvety texture.

1. **Tips for Achieving the Perfect Consistency**

- Consistency: Strive for a sauce that coats the back of a spoon evenly without being too thick or too thin. If the sauce is too thick, thin it with additional liquid; if too thin, simmer it longer to reduce and concentrate the flavors.
- Seasoning: Taste and adjust the seasoning of your sauce as needed, adding salt, pepper, herbs, or other flavorings to achieve a harmonious balance of flavors.
- Straining: For a silky-smooth texture, strain your sauce through a fine mesh sieve to remove any lumps or impurities. This step is particularly important for velvety sauces like hollandaise or béarnaise.

With these essential techniques at your fingertips, you're well-equipped to tackle the diverse array of sauces featured throughout this cookbook. So, roll up your sleeves, sharpen your knives, and let's dive into the delicious world of sauce-making!

Chapter 2: Classic French Sauces

In this chapter of "Sauce Secrets: A Restaurant Sauces Cookbook," we pay homage to the rich tradition of French cuisine with a focus on classic French sauces. These foundational sauces, including Béchamel, Velouté, Espagnole, Hollandaise, and more, form the cornerstone of French culinary artistry. We'll explore their origins, techniques for preparation, and offer creative variations to suit modern palates. Additionally, we'll provide expert pairing suggestions to elevate your meats, seafood, and vegetables to new heights of flavor and sophistication.

1. **Béchamel Sauce**

- Origin: Dating back to the 17th century, Béchamel sauce is a creamy white sauce made from a roux (butter and flour) and milk.
- Technique: Prepare a roux by melting butter in a saucepan, adding flour, and cooking until golden. Gradually whisk in warm milk until smooth and thickened. Season with salt, pepper, and nutmeg to taste.
- Variations: Enhance the flavor of Béchamel with additions such as grated cheese for Mornay sauce or mustard for a tangy twist. Incorporate fresh herbs like thyme or tarragon for a fragrant infusion.
- Pairing Suggestions: Béchamel is a versatile sauce that pairs beautifully with a variety of dishes, including gratins, pasta, and vegetable casseroles.

1. **Velouté Sauce**

- Origin: Velouté, meaning "velvety" in French, is a light sauce made from a roux and a light stock, such as chicken, fish, or veal.

- Technique: Prepare a roux with butter and flour, then gradually whisk in warmed stock until smooth and thickened. Simmer gently until the sauce reaches the desired consistency.
- Variations: Experiment with different stocks to create unique flavor profiles. Add cream for a richer texture or infuse the sauce with aromatics like shallots or garlic.
- Pairing Suggestions: Velouté sauce is a classic accompaniment to poached fish, poultry, and delicate vegetables such as asparagus or artichokes.

1. **Espagnole Sauce**

- Origin: Also known as brown sauce, Espagnole is a rich and hearty sauce made from brown stock, tomatoes, and brown roux.
- Technique: Begin by preparing a brown roux with equal parts butter and flour, then slowly whisk in brown stock and tomato paste. Simmer gently until the sauce thickens and the flavors meld.
- Variations: Add depth to Espagnole sauce with aromatic vegetables like carrots, onions, and celery. Incorporate red wine or brandy for complexity and richness.
- Pairing Suggestions: Espagnole sauce is a classic pairing with red meats such as beef or lamb, as well as roasted game birds like duck or pheasant.

1. **Hollandaise Sauce**

- Origin: Hollandaise sauce is a luxurious emulsion of egg yolks, butter, and lemon juice, believed to have originated in France but popularized in Holland.
- Technique: Whisk egg yolks with lemon juice over a double boiler until thickened, then slowly drizzle in melted butter,

whisking continuously until smooth and creamy. Season with salt and cayenne pepper to taste.

- Variations: Experiment with flavored variations of Hollandaise, such as adding tarragon or Dijon mustard for a subtle twist. Substitute clarified butter for a lighter, silkier texture.
- Pairing Suggestions: Hollandaise sauce is a classic accompaniment to eggs Benedict, steamed asparagus, and grilled seafood such as salmon or lobster.

Pairing Suggestions with Meats, Seafood, and Vegetables

- Meats: Pair Béchamel with baked chicken breast, Velouté with poached veal, Espagnole with braised beef short ribs, and Hollandaise with grilled steak or roasted lamb chops.
- Seafood: Serve Velouté with poached fish fillets, Espagnole with seared scallops, and Hollandaise with sautéed shrimp or crab cakes.
- Vegetables: Use Béchamel in vegetable gratins or lasagnas, Velouté in creamy mushroom sauces for pasta, Espagnole in ratatouille or vegetable stews, and Hollandaise drizzled over steamed or grilled vegetables like broccoli or green beans.

With these classic French sauces and expert pairing suggestions, you'll be well-equipped to recreate the timeless elegance of French cuisine in your own kitchen. Bon appétit!

Chapter 3: Italian Sauces

Welcome to the vibrant world of Italian cuisine! In this chapter of "Sauce Secrets: A Restaurant Sauces Cookbook," we explore the diverse array of Italian sauces that have captivated taste buds around the globe. From the classic Marinara to the indulgent Alfredo, the herbaceous Pesto to the hearty Bolognese, we'll uncover the secrets behind these iconic sauces and offer homemade recipes that celebrate the flavors of Italy's various regions. Get ready to savor the essence of Italian cooking with our expertly crafted sauces and serving ideas.

1. **Marinara Sauce**

   - Origin: Hailing from southern Italy, Marinara sauce is a simple yet flavorful tomato-based sauce seasoned with garlic, onions, and herbs.
   - Homemade Recipe: In a saucepan, sauté minced garlic and diced onions in olive oil until softened. Add crushed tomatoes, a splash of red wine (optional), and a pinch of sugar for balance. Simmer gently and season with salt, pepper, and fresh basil.
   - Serving Ideas: Serve Marinara sauce tossed with al dente spaghetti or layered in lasagna. It's also delicious as a dipping sauce for garlic bread or mozzarella sticks.

1. **Alfredo Sauce**

   - Origin: Alfredo sauce, known as "Fettuccine Alfredo" in Italy, originated in Rome. It's a rich and creamy sauce made from butter, heavy cream, and Parmesan cheese.
   - Homemade Recipe: In a saucepan, melt butter over medium heat, then whisk in heavy cream until warmed through. Gradually add grated Parmesan cheese, stirring until melted and

smooth. Season with salt, pepper, and a pinch of nutmeg.

- Serving Ideas: Toss Alfredo sauce with fettuccine pasta for a classic dish, or use it as a luxurious topping for grilled chicken or seafood.

3. Pesto Sauce

- Origin: Pesto sauce originates from the Liguria region of northern Italy and is traditionally made with fresh basil, pine nuts, garlic, Parmesan cheese, and olive oil.
- Homemade Recipe: In a food processor, combine fresh basil leaves, toasted pine nuts, minced garlic, grated Parmesan cheese, and extra virgin olive oil. Pulse until smooth, then season with salt and pepper to taste.
- Serving Ideas: Toss Pesto sauce with cooked pasta, spread it on bruschetta or sandwiches, or use it as a flavorful marinade for grilled vegetables or chicken.

1. Bolognese Sauce

- Origin: Bolognese sauce, or "Ragù alla Bolognese," hails from the Emilia-Romagna region of northern Italy. It's a hearty meat sauce made with ground beef, tomatoes, onions, carrots, celery, and aromatic herbs.
- Homemade Recipe: In a large skillet, brown ground beef in olive oil, then add diced onions, carrots, and celery. Cook until vegetables are softened, then add crushed tomatoes, tomato paste, and a splash of red wine. Simmer gently until flavors meld, then season with salt, pepper, and a pinch of nutmeg.
- Serving Ideas: Serve Bolognese sauce tossed with tagliatelle or pappardelle pasta, or use it as a filling for lasagna or stuffed peppers.

Regional Specialties and Unique Ingredients

- Amatriciana: Originating from the town of Amatrice in Lazio, this spicy tomato sauce is flavored with pancetta or guanciale (cured pork cheek) and pecorino cheese.
- Carbonara: A Roman specialty, Carbonara sauce is made with eggs, Pecorino Romano cheese, pancetta, and black pepper, creating a rich and creamy pasta sauce.
- Puttanesca: This bold and flavorful sauce from Naples is made with tomatoes, olives, capers, garlic, and anchovies, creating a savory and briny flavor profile.

Homemade Pasta Sauce Recipes and Serving Ideas

- Arrabbiata Sauce: A spicy tomato sauce flavored with garlic and red pepper flakes, perfect for adding a kick to pasta dishes.
- Cacio e Pepe: A simple yet elegant sauce made with Pecorino Romano cheese and black pepper, creating a creamy and peppery pasta sauce.
- Vodka Sauce: A creamy tomato sauce flavored with vodka, heavy cream, and Parmesan cheese, creating a rich and indulgent pasta sauce.

With these homemade Italian sauce recipes and serving ideas, you can bring the flavors of Italy to your table and experience the rich culinary heritage of this beloved cuisine. Buon appetito!

Chapter 4: Asian-Inspired Sauces

Prepare to embark on a culinary journey through the vibrant flavors of Asia in "Sauce Secrets: A Restaurant Sauces Cookbook." In this chapter, we explore a tantalizing array of Asian-inspired sauces that bring bold and distinctive flavors to your table. From the savory Soy-Ginger Glaze to the sweet and tangy Teriyaki, the zesty Sweet and Sour to the creamy Peanut Sauce, we'll uncover the secrets behind these beloved sauces and offer fusion recipes that blend Asian flavors with Western dishes. Get ready to experience the harmonious balance of sweet, sour, salty, and umami flavors that define Asian cuisine.

1. Soy-Ginger Glaze

- Origin: Inspired by Japanese and Chinese cuisines, Soy-Ginger Glaze is a versatile sauce made with soy sauce, ginger, garlic, and a touch of sweetness.
- Recipe: In a saucepan, combine soy sauce, grated ginger, minced garlic, brown sugar, rice vinegar, and a splash of sesame oil. Simmer until thickened, then use as a glaze for grilled meats, seafood, or vegetables.

2. Teriyaki Sauce

- Origin: Teriyaki sauce originated in Japan and is known for its sweet and savory flavor profile, typically made with soy sauce, mirin, sake, and sugar.
- Recipe: In a saucepan, combine soy sauce, mirin, sake (or dry sherry), brown sugar, and minced garlic. Simmer until the sauce thickens, then use it to marinate and glaze meats, tofu, or vegetables.

3. Sweet and Sour Sauce

- Origin: Sweet and Sour sauce is a popular condiment in Chinese cuisine, featuring a balance of sweetness from sugar and tanginess from vinegar, often enhanced with ketchup and pineapple.
- Recipe: In a saucepan, combine pineapple juice, rice vinegar, ketchup, brown sugar, and soy sauce. Bring to a simmer, then thicken with a cornstarch slurry. Add diced bell peppers, onions, and pineapple chunks for texture and flavor.

4. Peanut Sauce

- Origin: Peanut Sauce, also known as Satay Sauce, is a creamy and flavorful sauce commonly found in Southeast Asian cuisines, made with peanut butter, coconut milk, soy sauce, and spices.
- Recipe: In a blender, combine peanut butter, coconut milk, soy sauce, lime juice, garlic, ginger, and a touch of honey or brown sugar. Blend until smooth, then adjust the seasoning with salt and chili flakes for heat.

Incorporating Umami-Rich Ingredients

- Miso: Add depth of flavor to sauces with fermented soybean paste, such as Miso, which brings a rich umami taste to dishes like Miso-glazed salmon or Miso soup.
- Fish Sauce: Enhance the savory profile of sauces with Fish Sauce, a staple ingredient in Southeast Asian cooking, adding complexity and depth of flavor to dishes like Vietnamese dipping sauces or Thai curries.

Fusion Recipes Blending Asian Flavors with Western Dishes

- Asian-inspired BBQ Sauce: Blend Asian flavors like soy sauce, ginger, and sesame oil with traditional BBQ sauce ingredients for a unique twist on classic barbecue dishes.

- Soy-Ginger Marinade for Grilled Steak: Infuse Western-style steaks with Asian-inspired flavors by marinating them in a mixture of soy sauce, ginger, garlic, and brown sugar before grilling.
- Teriyaki Chicken Pizza: Combine the flavors of Teriyaki sauce with Western pizza toppings like chicken, bell peppers, and pineapple for a delicious fusion dish.

With these Asian-inspired sauce recipes and fusion ideas, you can explore the diverse and exciting flavors of Asian cuisine while adding a unique twist to your favorite Western dishes. Get ready to tantalize your taste buds and embark on a culinary adventure like no other!

Chapter 5: Latin American Sauces

Bienvenidos a la vibrante cocina latinoamericana! In this chapter of "Sauce Secrets: A Restaurant Sauces Cookbook," we explore the bold and diverse flavors of Latin America through a selection of iconic sauces. From the zesty Salsa Verde to the herbaceous Chimichurri, the complex Mole to the fiery Aji Amarillo, we'll uncover the secrets behind these beloved sauces and showcase authentic recipes from various Latin American countries. Get ready to spice up your meals with these spicy and vibrant sauces, perfect for tacos, grilled meats, seafood, and beyond.

1. Salsa Verde

- Origin: Salsa Verde, or "green sauce," is a tangy and versatile condiment popular throughout Latin America. It typically features tomatillos, chili peppers, onions, cilantro, and lime juice.
- Authentic Recipe: In a blender, combine roasted tomatillos, jalapeños or serrano peppers, diced onions, minced garlic, fresh cilantro, lime juice, and salt. Blend until smooth, then adjust seasoning to taste.

2. Chimichurri

- Origin: Chimichurri is a vibrant and herbaceous sauce originating from Argentina and Uruguay, commonly used as a marinade or condiment for grilled meats.
- Authentic Recipe: In a bowl, combine chopped parsley, minced garlic, red wine vinegar, olive oil, oregano, and red pepper flakes. Let the flavors meld for at least 30 minutes before serving.

3. Mole

- Origin: Mole is a complex and rich sauce originating from Mexico, known for its combination of chili peppers, chocolate, spices, and other ingredients.
- Authentic Recipe: There are many variations of Mole, but a traditional recipe may include dried chili peppers (such as ancho, pasilla, and mulato), tomatoes, onions, garlic, spices (such as cinnamon, cloves, and cumin), chocolate, and nuts (such as almonds or peanuts), all simmered together until thickened and flavorful.

4. Aji Amarillo

- Origin: Aji Amarillo, or "yellow chili," is a spicy and fruity chili pepper commonly used in Peruvian cuisine, particularly in sauces and marinades.
- Authentic Recipe: In a blender, combine Aji Amarillo peppers (seeds removed for less heat), diced onions, garlic, lime juice, olive oil, and salt. Blend until smooth, then adjust seasoning to taste.

Authentic Recipes from Various Latin American Countries

- Pebre (Chile): A fresh and spicy Chilean salsa made with tomatoes, onions, cilantro, garlic, and chili peppers, often served with bread or grilled meats.
- Cilantro Mojo (Cuba): A tangy and herbaceous Cuban sauce made with fresh cilantro, garlic, lime juice, and olive oil, perfect for marinating meats or drizzling over rice and beans.
- Salsa Criolla (Argentina): A simple and flavorful Argentine sauce made with sliced onions, red wine vinegar, olive oil, and chopped parsley, often served as a condiment for grilled meats.
- Salsa Lizano (Costa Rica): A unique and tangy Costa Rican sauce made with vegetables, spices, and vinegar, commonly used

as a condiment for rice and beans, empanadas, and other dishes.

With these authentic Latin American sauce recipes, you can bring the vibrant flavors of the region into your kitchen and elevate your dishes with a touch of Latino flair. Whether you're grilling meats, preparing tacos, or simply dipping chips, these spicy and vibrant sauces are sure to delight your taste buds and transport you to the streets of Latin America. ¡Buen provecho!

Chapter 6: Global Fusion Sauces

Prepare to embark on a culinary adventure that transcends borders and embraces a world of flavors in "Sauce Secrets: A Restaurant Sauces Cookbook." In this chapter, we celebrate the art of fusion cuisine by exploring cross-cultural blends and innovative flavor combinations that push the boundaries of traditional sauce-making. From East-meets-West concoctions to creative interpretations of global classics, we'll showcase recipes inspired by international travels, culinary trends, and the spirit of culinary experimentation. Get ready to embark on a flavor-filled journey that knows no limits!

1. Thai Peanut BBQ Sauce

- Inspiration: Drawing inspiration from Thai and American barbecue traditions, this sauce combines the rich nuttiness of peanut sauce with the smoky sweetness of BBQ sauce.
- Recipe: In a saucepan, combine peanut butter, soy sauce, brown sugar, lime juice, minced garlic, ginger, and chili flakes. Simmer until thickened, then brush onto grilled meats or use as a dipping sauce for skewers.

2. Mediterranean Chimichurri

- Inspiration: Putting a Mediterranean twist on the classic Argentine Chimichurri, this sauce incorporates ingredients like sun-dried tomatoes, Kalamata olives, and feta cheese for a burst of Mediterranean flavor.
- Recipe: In a food processor, blend fresh parsley, cilantro, sun-dried tomatoes, Kalamata olives, garlic, red wine vinegar, olive oil, and crumbled feta cheese until smooth. Use as a marinade for grilled chicken or a topping for roasted vegetables.

3. Korean BBQ Teriyaki Glaze

- Inspiration: Combining the bold flavors of Korean BBQ with the sweet and savory profile of Japanese Teriyaki sauce, this glaze adds a unique twist to grilled meats and seafood.
- Recipe: In a saucepan, combine soy sauce, brown sugar, sesame oil, minced garlic, grated ginger, and Korean chili paste (gochujang). Simmer until thickened, then brush onto grilled meats or seafood for a flavorful finish.

4. Mexican Sriracha Ranch

- Inspiration: Taking inspiration from both Mexican and American cuisines, this creamy Sriracha Ranch sauce combines the coolness of ranch dressing with the fiery kick of Sriracha hot sauce.
- Recipe: In a bowl, whisk together mayonnaise, sour cream, buttermilk, minced garlic, chopped cilantro, lime juice, and Sriracha hot sauce. Season with salt and pepper to taste. Serve as a dipping sauce for tacos, chicken wings, or vegetable crudité.

Experimentation with Ingredients from Different Cuisines

- Wasabi Lime Mayo: Combine Japanese wasabi paste with zesty lime juice and creamy mayo for a tangy and spicy condiment perfect for sushi rolls or fish tacos.
- Curry Coconut Aioli: Blend Indian curry powder with coconut milk and garlic-infused mayo for a creamy and aromatic aioli that pairs beautifully with sweet potato fries or crispy shrimp.

Recipes Inspired by International Travels and Culinary Trends

- Harissa Honey Glaze: Inspired by the bold flavors of North African cuisine, this glaze combines spicy harissa paste with sweet honey for a versatile sauce that adds depth to grilled meats, vegetables, or even pizza.

- Gochujang Maple Syrup: Drawing inspiration from Korean cuisine, this sweet and spicy sauce combines fermented gochujang paste with maple syrup for a unique glaze or dipping sauce that's perfect for chicken wings or glazed vegetables.

With these global fusion sauce recipes, you can embark on a culinary journey that celebrates the diverse flavors of the world while encouraging creativity and experimentation in the kitchen. So, grab your passport and get ready to explore the exciting world of fusion cuisine!

Chapter 7: Vegan and Gluten-Free Sauces

Welcome to a chapter dedicated to delicious and inclusive sauces that cater to a variety of dietary preferences and restrictions. In "Sauce Secrets: A Restaurant Sauces Cookbook," we celebrate the creativity and versatility of vegan and gluten-free sauces, offering dairy-free cream sauces, plant-based gravies, and more. Whether you're following a vegan lifestyle, avoiding gluten, or simply looking to incorporate more plant-based options into your diet, these sauces are sure to satisfy your cravings and elevate your meals.

1. Creamy Cashew Alfredo Sauce

- Description: Indulge in the rich and creamy flavors of Alfredo sauce without any dairy. This vegan version substitutes cashews for cream, resulting in a luscious sauce that's perfect for tossing with pasta or drizzling over vegetables.
- Recipe: In a blender, combine soaked cashews, nutritional yeast, garlic, lemon juice, vegetable broth, and salt. Blend until smooth and creamy. Heat the sauce gently in a saucepan before serving.

2. Mushroom Gravy

- Description: This hearty and flavorful gravy is made from mushrooms and vegetable broth, offering a vegan alternative to traditional meat-based gravies. Serve it over mashed potatoes, roasted vegetables, or vegan meat substitutes.
- Recipe: In a skillet, sauté chopped mushrooms, onions, and garlic until golden brown. Add vegetable broth, soy sauce, thyme, and a cornstarch slurry to thicken the gravy. Season with salt and pepper to taste.

3. Roasted Red Pepper Pesto

- Description: Elevate your pasta dishes with this vibrant and flavorful pesto made from roasted red peppers, basil, garlic, and nuts. It's a dairy-free and gluten-free alternative to traditional basil pesto, perfect for tossing with gluten-free pasta or using as a spread.
- Recipe: In a food processor, combine roasted red peppers, fresh basil leaves, garlic, pine nuts (or almonds), nutritional yeast, and olive oil. Blend until smooth, then season with salt and pepper to taste.

4. Coconut Curry Sauce

- Description: Experience the exotic flavors of curry with this creamy and aromatic sauce made from coconut milk, curry paste, and spices. It's a versatile sauce that pairs beautifully with tofu, vegetables, or grains like rice or quinoa.
- Recipe: In a saucepan, combine coconut milk, red or green curry paste, minced garlic, ginger, and a splash of lime juice. Simmer gently until the sauce thickens and the flavors meld. Adjust seasoning with salt and sugar if needed.

Creative Substitutions for Gluten-Containing Ingredients

- Tamari or Coconut Aminos: Substitute soy sauce with gluten-free alternatives like tamari or coconut aminos to add savory flavor to your sauces without the gluten.
- Cornstarch or Arrowroot: Use cornstarch or arrowroot powder as a thickening agent instead of wheat flour to achieve the desired consistency in your sauces.

Recipes Suitable for a Variety of Dietary Preferences and Restrictions

- Cilantro Lime Crema: Combine dairy-free yogurt with lime

juice, cilantro, and a pinch of salt to create a tangy and refreshing sauce that's perfect for tacos, burrito bowls, or grilled vegetables.

- Tahini Lemon Dressing: Whisk together tahini, lemon juice, garlic, and water to create a creamy and zesty dressing that's ideal for drizzling over salads or roasted vegetables.

With these vegan and gluten-free sauce recipes, you can enjoy the flavors and versatility of sauces without compromising on your dietary preferences or restrictions. Whether you're following a plant-based lifestyle, avoiding gluten, or simply looking to add more variety to your meals, these sauces are sure to delight your taste buds and inspire your culinary creativity.

Chapter 8: Dessert Sauces and Condiments

Indulge your sweet tooth and elevate your desserts to new heights with a delectable array of dessert sauces and condiments in "Sauce Secrets: A Restaurant Sauces Cookbook." From luxurious Chocolate Ganache to decadent Caramel Sauce, vibrant Fruit Coulis, and more, this chapter celebrates the art of sweet sauces that add flair and flavor to your favorite treats. Whether drizzling over ice cream, dipping fresh fruit, or layering in cakes and pastries, these versatile sauces are sure to delight your taste buds and enhance your dining experience.

1. Chocolate Ganache

- Description: Smooth, rich, and velvety, chocolate ganache is a classic dessert sauce made from chocolate and cream. It's perfect for topping cakes, cupcakes, or brownies, or for dipping fruits and pastries.
- Recipe: Heat heavy cream until steaming, then pour it over finely chopped chocolate. Let it sit for a few minutes, then whisk until smooth and glossy. Adjust the ratio of cream to chocolate to achieve the desired consistency.

2. Caramel Sauce

- Description: Indulge in the sweet and buttery goodness of caramel sauce, perfect for drizzling over ice cream, pancakes, or apple pie, or for dipping sliced apples or pretzels.
- Recipe: In a saucepan, melt sugar over medium heat until golden brown. Remove from heat and slowly whisk in warm heavy cream and butter until smooth. Be careful, as the mixture will bubble up.

3. Fruit Coulis

- Description: Vibrant and refreshing, fruit coulis is a puree made from fresh or frozen fruits, sweetened and strained to a smooth consistency. It's ideal for drizzling over cheesecake, panna cotta, or yogurt, or for swirling into cocktails or mocktails.
- Recipe: In a blender, combine fresh or thawed frozen fruits with a touch of sugar or honey and lemon juice. Blend until smooth, then strain through a fine mesh sieve to remove any seeds or pulp.

4. Raspberry Balsamic Reduction

- Description: Tangy and slightly sweet, raspberry balsamic reduction is a versatile sauce that pairs beautifully with desserts like vanilla ice cream, cheesecake, or pound cake, or even with savory dishes like roasted vegetables or grilled meats.
- Recipe: In a saucepan, simmer fresh raspberries with balsamic vinegar and sugar until thickened and syrupy. Strain the mixture to remove seeds, if desired, then let it cool before using.

Tips for Presentation and Garnishing to Enhance the Dining Experience

- Drizzling: Use a spoon or a squeeze bottle to create elegant drizzles or decorative patterns on plates or desserts, adding visual appeal and a touch of sophistication.
- Garnishing: Garnish desserts with fresh fruit, edible flowers, chopped nuts, or chocolate shavings to add texture, color, and contrast to your creations.
- Layering: Create visually stunning desserts by layering different sauces and textures, such as alternating layers of chocolate ganache and caramel sauce in a parfait or trifle.
- Dusting: Dust desserts with powdered sugar, cocoa powder, or

ground spices like cinnamon or nutmeg for a finishing touch that adds flavor and elegance.

With these sumptuous dessert sauce recipes and presentation tips, you can transform ordinary desserts into extraordinary culinary creations that dazzle the senses and delight the palate. Whether you're hosting a dinner party or simply treating yourself to a sweet indulgence, these sauces are sure to be the perfect finishing touch to any dessert masterpiece.

Chapter 9: Mediterranean Sauces

Welcome to the sun-drenched shores of the Mediterranean, where the cuisine is celebrated for its vibrant flavors and fresh ingredients. In this chapter of "Sauce Secrets: A Restaurant Sauces Cookbook," we explore the rich tapestry of Mediterranean sauces, from the creamy Tzatziki to the smoky Romesco, the fiery Harissa to the garlicky Aioli, and more. These sauces are the perfect accompaniments for grilled meats, vegetables, and mezze platters, adding depth and complexity to every bite. Join us as we delve into the techniques for incorporating fresh herbs and spices to create authentic Mediterranean delights that will transport you to the shores of Greece, Spain, and beyond.

1. Tzatziki

- Description: Cool and refreshing, Tzatziki is a Greek yogurt sauce flavored with cucumbers, garlic, lemon juice, and fresh dill or mint. It's the perfect accompaniment for grilled meats, gyros, or as a dip for pita bread and vegetables.
- Technique: Grate cucumbers and squeeze out excess moisture, then mix them with Greek yogurt, minced garlic, lemon juice, chopped dill or mint, and a drizzle of olive oil. Season with salt and pepper to taste.

2. Romesco Sauce

- Description: Hailing from Catalonia, Spain, Romesco sauce is a rich and smoky sauce made from roasted red peppers, tomatoes, almonds, and garlic. It's traditionally served with grilled vegetables, seafood, or crusty bread.
- Technique: Roast red peppers and tomatoes until charred, then blend them with toasted almonds, garlic, sherry vinegar, smoked paprika, and olive oil until smooth. Adjust seasoning

with salt and pepper.

3. Harissa

- Description: Harissa is a fiery and aromatic chili paste commonly used in North African and Mediterranean cuisines. Made from roasted red peppers, chili peppers, garlic, and spices, it adds heat and depth to dishes like grilled meats, couscous, or hummus.
- Technique: Blend roasted red peppers, dried chili peppers, garlic, cumin, coriander, caraway seeds, and olive oil until smooth. Adjust the level of heat by adding more or fewer chili peppers.

4. Aioli

- Description: Aioli is a garlicky mayonnaise-based sauce that originated in the Mediterranean region, particularly in Provence, France, and Catalonia, Spain. It's often flavored with garlic, lemon juice, and fresh herbs like basil or parsley.
- Technique: Whisk together mayonnaise, minced garlic, lemon juice, and chopped herbs until smooth and well combined. Adjust seasoning with salt and pepper to taste.

Techniques for Incorporating Fresh Herbs and Spices

- Chopping: Finely chop fresh herbs like parsley, cilantro, dill, or mint to release their flavors and aromas, adding brightness and freshness to your sauces.
- Muddling: Use a mortar and pestle to muddle fresh herbs and spices like garlic, peppercorns, or coriander seeds, releasing their essential oils and intensifying their flavors.
- Infusing: Infuse olive oil with fresh herbs and spices by heating them gently in the oil over low heat, then straining out the solids. This creates a fragrant and flavorful base for your sauces.
- Toasting: Toast nuts and spices like almonds, cumin, or coriander seeds in a dry skillet until fragrant and golden brown, then grind them into a fine powder or paste to add depth and complexity to your sauces.

With these techniques and recipes for Mediterranean sauces, you can bring the flavors of the Mediterranean to your table and create authentic dishes that celebrate the vibrant culinary traditions of the region. Whether you're grilling meats, vegetables, or serving up a mezze platter, these sauces are sure to add a burst of flavor and a touch of Mediterranean magic to every bite. Bon appétit!

Chapter 10: American BBQ Sauces

Welcome to the heartland of American barbecue, where the smoke rises and the flavors are bold and savory. In this chapter of "Sauce Secrets: A Restaurant Sauces Cookbook," we dive into the diverse world of American BBQ sauces, exploring the distinctive styles of Kansas City, Memphis, Carolina, and Texas. From the sweet and tangy sauces of Kansas City to the dry-rubbed ribs of Memphis, the vinegar-based sauces of Carolina to the peppery and robust flavors of Texas, each region offers its own unique twist on this beloved culinary tradition. Join us as we explore the slow-cooked, smoky flavors and tangy tomato bases that define American BBQ, with recipes for ribs, pulled pork, chicken, and more.

1. Kansas City BBQ Sauce

- Description: Sweet, smoky, and thick, Kansas City BBQ sauce is a tomato-based sauce sweetened with molasses or brown sugar and flavored with vinegar, spices, and sometimes a hint of heat.
- Recipe: In a saucepan, combine ketchup, brown sugar, apple cider vinegar, Worcestershire sauce, mustard, paprika, garlic powder, onion powder, and cayenne pepper. Simmer until thickened, then adjust seasoning to taste.

2. Memphis Dry Rub

- Description: In Memphis, BBQ is all about the dry rub. This spice blend features a combination of paprika, brown sugar, garlic powder, onion powder, cumin, and other spices, creating a flavorful crust on ribs, pork shoulder, or chicken.
- Recipe: Mix together paprika, brown sugar, garlic powder, onion powder, cumin, chili powder, salt, and black pepper. Rub

the mixture generously onto the meat, then let it sit for several hours or overnight before smoking or grilling.

3. Carolina Vinegar Sauce

- Description: In the Carolinas, BBQ sauce is all about the vinegar. This thin and tangy sauce is made from apple cider vinegar, ketchup, brown sugar, and spices, adding a bright and tangy flavor to pulled pork or grilled chicken.
- Recipe: In a saucepan, combine apple cider vinegar, ketchup, brown sugar, red pepper flakes, black pepper, and salt. Simmer until slightly thickened, then let it cool before using.

4. Texas BBQ Sauce

- Description: Texas BBQ sauce is bold and robust, with a tomato base and a kick of heat from chili powder, cayenne pepper, or hot sauce. It's perfect for brisket, sausage, or beef ribs.
- Recipe: In a saucepan, combine ketchup, molasses, apple cider vinegar, chili powder, garlic powder, onion powder, cayenne pepper, and hot sauce. Simmer until thickened, then adjust seasoning to taste.

Recipes for Ribs, Pulled Pork, Chicken, and More

- Kansas City Baby Back Ribs: Rub baby back ribs with a Kansas City-style dry rub, then smoke or grill until tender. Brush with Kansas City BBQ sauce during the last 30 minutes of cooking for a sticky, sweet finish.
- Memphis Pulled Pork: Rub a pork shoulder with Memphis dry rub, then slow-cook it until tender and juicy. Serve with extra dry rub for sprinkling and Carolina vinegar sauce for drizzling.
- Carolina Pulled Chicken: Season chicken thighs with salt and pepper, then grill or roast until cooked through. Shred the

chicken and toss it with Carolina vinegar sauce for a tangy and flavorful dish.

- Texas Beef Brisket: Rub a beef brisket with Texas dry rub, then smoke it low and slow until tender. Slice thinly and serve with Texas BBQ sauce on the side for dipping or drizzling.

With these American BBQ sauce recipes and techniques, you can bring the flavors of the American South to your backyard grill or kitchen. Whether you're smoking ribs, pulling pork, or grilling chicken, these sauces are sure to add an extra layer of flavor and authenticity to your BBQ creations. So fire up the smoker, gather your friends and family, and get ready to enjoy the smoky, savory delights of American BBQ!

Chapter 11: Seafood Sauces

Dive into the bountiful world of seafood sauces in "Sauce Secrets: A Restaurant Sauces Cookbook." In this chapter, we explore a variety of sauces that enhance the natural flavors of fish and shellfish, from the classic Lemon Butter to the tangy Tartar Sauce, the zesty Cocktail Sauce, and beyond. Whether you're grilling, baking, or frying your seafood, these sauces are the perfect accompaniments, adding depth and brightness to every bite. Join us as we discover the art of pairing sauces with different types of seafood and creating memorable dining experiences that celebrate the ocean's bounty.

1. Lemon Butter Sauce

- Description: Simple yet elegant, Lemon Butter sauce is a classic accompaniment to fish and seafood. Made with butter, lemon juice, and fresh herbs, it adds richness and tanginess to grilled or pan-seared fish.
- Pairing: Pair with delicate white fish such as sole, flounder, or trout, as well as shellfish like shrimp or scallops.

2. Tartar Sauce

- Description: Creamy and tangy, Tartar Sauce is a mayonnaise-based sauce flavored with pickles, capers, and herbs. It's the perfect condiment for fried seafood like fish and chips or crab cakes.
- Pairing: Serve with fried fish, shrimp, or oysters, as well as seafood sandwiches or wraps.

3. Cocktail Sauce

- Description: Bold and spicy, Cocktail Sauce is a tomato-based sauce flavored with horseradish, lemon juice, Worcestershire sauce, and hot sauce. It's the classic accompaniment for chilled seafood like shrimp cocktail or raw oysters.

- Pairing: Serve with chilled shrimp, crab claws, raw oysters, or seafood platters for a refreshing and zesty kick.

4. Remoulade Sauce

- Description: Creamy and tangy, Remoulade Sauce is a mayonnaise-based sauce flavored with mustard, capers, herbs, and spices. It's versatile and can be served as a dip, dressing, or spread for a variety of seafood dishes.
- Pairing: Serve with fried seafood like catfish, soft-shell crab, or shrimp po'boys, as well as crab cakes or fish tacos.

Pairing Suggestions with Different Types of Seafood

- Grilled Salmon with Dill Butter: Pair grilled salmon fillets with a creamy Dill Butter sauce made with butter, lemon juice, and fresh dill for a bright and flavorful dish.
- Pan-Seared Scallops with Beurre Blanc: Serve pan-seared scallops with a classic Beurre Blanc sauce made with white wine, shallots, butter, and lemon juice for an elegant and indulgent meal.
- Fried Calamari with Aioli: Accompany fried calamari rings with a garlicky Aioli sauce made with mayonnaise, garlic, lemon juice, and olive oil for a Mediterranean-inspired appetizer.
- Grilled Shrimp with Chimichurri: Pair grilled shrimp skewers with a vibrant Chimichurri sauce made with fresh herbs, garlic, vinegar, and olive oil for a burst of flavor.

With these seafood sauce recipes and pairing suggestions, you can create memorable dining experiences that celebrate the fresh flavors of the ocean. Whether you're hosting a dinner party or enjoying a cozy meal at home, these sauces are sure to elevate your seafood dishes and delight your taste buds. So grab your apron and get ready to dive into a world of delicious seafood sauces!

Chapter 12: Breakfast and Brunch Sauces

Start your day off right with a delicious array of breakfast and brunch sauces in "Sauce Secrets: A Restaurant Sauces Cookbook." In this chapter, we explore morning-friendly sauces designed to kickstart your day, from the classic Hollandaise for Eggs Benedict to the sweet Maple Syrup for Pancakes, and beyond. Whether you're hosting a leisurely brunch with friends or treating yourself to a special breakfast at home, these creative sauce recipes are sure to add flair and flavor to your morning routine.

1. Hollandaise Sauce

- Description: Smooth, buttery, and rich, Hollandaise sauce is a classic brunch staple, perfect for drizzling over Eggs Benedict, asparagus, or steamed vegetables.
- Morning Pairing: Serve with poached eggs, Canadian bacon, and English muffins for a traditional Eggs Benedict, or use as a topping for steamed asparagus or broccoli.

2. Maple Syrup

- Description: Sweet and golden, maple syrup is a beloved accompaniment to pancakes, waffles, French toast, and other breakfast delights, adding a touch of warmth and sweetness to every bite.
- Morning Pairing: Drizzle over a stack of fluffy pancakes or crispy Belgian waffles, or use as a dipping sauce for French toast sticks or breakfast sausages.

3. Berry Compote

- Description: Bursting with fresh fruit flavor, berry compote is a vibrant and versatile sauce made from simmering berries with sugar and lemon juice until thick and syrupy. It's perfect for topping pancakes, yogurt, oatmeal, or cheesecake.

- Morning Pairing: Spoon over a stack of buttermilk pancakes or Greek yogurt parfait, or swirl into oatmeal or porridge for a fruity burst of flavor.

4. Avocado Crema

- Description: Creamy and tangy, avocado crema is a refreshing sauce made from ripe avocados, sour cream or Greek yogurt, lime juice, cilantro, and spices. It's a delicious accompaniment to breakfast tacos, huevos rancheros, or breakfast burritos.
- Morning Pairing: Dollop onto scrambled eggs or breakfast tacos, or use as a spread for toast or bagels topped with smoked salmon and sliced tomatoes.

Creative Brunch Sauce Recipes for Special Occasions

- Champagne Berry Sauce: Simmer mixed berries with champagne, sugar, and lemon zest until reduced into a luscious sauce, perfect for spooning over Belgian waffles or angel food cake for a special brunch celebration.
- Lemon Ricotta Cream: Blend ricotta cheese with honey, lemon zest, and vanilla extract until smooth and creamy, creating a luxurious topping for pancakes, French toast, or crepes.
- Spicy Sriracha Mayo: Mix mayonnaise with Sriracha hot sauce, lime juice, and honey for a spicy and tangy sauce that adds a kick to breakfast sandwiches, hash browns, or avocado toast.
- Cinnamon Brown Butter: Brown butter with cinnamon and maple syrup until fragrant and nutty, then drizzle over cinnamon rolls, baked oatmeal, or grilled peaches for a decadent brunch treat.

With these breakfast and brunch sauce recipes, you can elevate your morning meals and create memorable dining experiences that celebrate the joy of starting the day with delicious flavors and comforting dishes. Whether you're hosting a casual weekend brunch or treating yourself to a special breakfast at home, these sauces are sure to make every morning a little brighter. So grab your favorite breakfast foods and get ready to enjoy a delicious start to your day!

Chapter 13: Healthy and Light Sauces

In this chapter of "Sauce Secrets: A Restaurant Sauces Cookbook," we embrace the art of creating healthy and light sauces that don't compromise on flavor. From yogurt-based dressings to citrus vinaigrettes and herb-infused sauces, these recipes offer low-calorie options perfect for those looking to enjoy delicious sauces without the guilt. Join us as we explore techniques for reducing fat and sugar content while maintaining taste, ensuring that every dish is as nutritious as it is flavorful.

1. Greek Yogurt Tzatziki Dressing

- Description: Creamy and tangy, this Greek yogurt-based dressing is flavored with cucumber, garlic, lemon juice, and dill. It's perfect for drizzling over salads, grilled vegetables, or falafel bowls.
- Healthy Twist: Substitute Greek yogurt for mayonnaise or sour cream to reduce fat content while still enjoying a creamy texture and tangy flavor.

2. Citrus Vinaigrette

- Description: Light and refreshing, citrus vinaigrette is made with fresh lemon or orange juice, olive oil, Dijon mustard, and honey or maple syrup for a touch of sweetness. It's ideal for dressing salads, roasted vegetables, or grilled seafood.
- Healthy Twist: Use a smaller amount of olive oil and sweetener to reduce calories while still achieving a balanced and flavorful dressing.

3. Herb-infused Chimichurri Sauce

- Description: Bursting with fresh herbs like parsley, cilantro, and oregano, chimichurri sauce is a vibrant and aromatic condiment perfect for grilled meats, seafood, or roasted vegetables.

- Healthy Twist: Increase the proportion of fresh herbs to oil and vinegar to reduce fat content while maximizing flavor and nutrition.

Tips for Reducing Fat and Sugar Content While Maintaining Taste

- Use Natural Sweeteners: Opt for natural sweeteners like honey, maple syrup, or fruit juices instead of refined sugar to add sweetness to sauces without adding empty calories.
- Choose Healthy Fats: Use heart-healthy fats like olive oil, avocado oil, or nut oils in moderation to reduce saturated fat content while still providing flavor and richness.
- Incorporate Fresh Herbs and Spices: Boost flavor without adding extra calories by using plenty of fresh herbs, garlic, onions, and spices in your sauces.
- Experiment with Vinegars and Citrus Juices: Use vinegars and citrus juices to add acidity and brightness to sauces without relying on excessive amounts of oil or salt.

With these healthy and light sauce recipes and tips, you can enjoy delicious flavors without sacrificing your health or dietary goals. Whether you're dressing salads, marinating meats, or dipping vegetables, these sauces are sure to add a burst of flavor to every meal.

Chapter 14: Comfort Food Sauces

Indulge in the comforting flavors of childhood favorites with the recipes in this chapter of "Sauce Secrets: A Restaurant Sauces Cookbook." From creamy macaroni and cheese sauce to rich gravy and hearty tomato soup base, these sauces evoke nostalgia and warmth, perfect for cozy meals on chilly evenings or rainy days. Join us as we explore the beloved flavors of comfort food and share cozy recipes that are sure to bring comfort and joy to your table.

1. Macaroni and Cheese Sauce

- Description: Creamy and indulgent, macaroni and cheese sauce is a beloved comfort food classic. Made with a combination of cheese, milk, and butter, it's the perfect sauce for coating tender pasta shells or elbows.
- Nostalgic Flavors: Recreate the nostalgic flavors of childhood with this rich and cheesy sauce that's sure to bring back memories of family dinners and special occasions.

2. Gravy

- Description: Rich and savory, gravy is a staple sauce that adds depth and flavor to a variety of comfort foods, from mashed potatoes and roasted meats to biscuits and fried chicken.
- Nostalgic Flavors: Whether it's smothering a plate of fluffy mashed potatoes or dripping over a slice of juicy roast beef, gravy is the ultimate comfort food sauce that brings warmth and satisfaction with every bite.

3. Tomato Soup Base

- Description: Hearty and comforting, tomato soup base is the perfect starting point for a cozy bowl of soup on a chilly day.

Made with ripe tomatoes, onions, garlic, and herbs, it's a classic comfort food that's both soothing and satisfying.

- Nostalgic Flavors: There's nothing quite like a bowl of tomato soup on a rainy day, served with a grilled cheese sandwich for dipping. With its rich tomato flavor and aromatic herbs, this soup base is sure to evoke memories of childhood lunches and family gatherings.

Cozy Recipes for Chilly Evenings or Rainy Days

- Homemade Macaroni and Cheese: Toss cooked macaroni with homemade cheese sauce made from sharp cheddar, milk, butter, and a hint of mustard powder. Bake until bubbly and golden for a comforting dish that's perfect for a cozy night in.
- Roast Beef with Gravy: Serve slices of tender roast beef with rich and savory gravy made from pan drippings, beef broth, and flour. Pair with mashed potatoes and roasted vegetables for a hearty and satisfying meal.
- Creamy Tomato Basil Soup: Simmer ripe tomatoes with onions, garlic, and fresh basil until tender, then blend until smooth and creamy. Serve with a dollop of sour cream and a sprinkle of fresh basil for a comforting bowl of soup that's perfect for rainy days.
- Biscuits and Gravy: Serve fluffy biscuits smothered in creamy sausage gravy made from breakfast sausage, flour, milk, and seasonings for a classic Southern comfort food dish that's sure to warm you up on chilly mornings.

With these comforting sauce recipes and cozy meal ideas, you can create memorable dining experiences that bring warmth and nostalgia to your table. Whether you're craving macaroni and cheese, gravy, or tomato soup, these comforting sauces are sure to satisfy your cravings and lift your spirits on even the gloomiest of days.

Chapter 15: Fermented Sauces and Condiments

Step into the world of fermentation with the recipes in this chapter of "Sauce Secrets: A Restaurant Sauces Cookbook." From tangy kimchi to classic sauerkraut and fiery hot sauce, fermented sauces and condiments add depth of flavor and beneficial probiotics to dishes, enhancing both taste and nutrition. Join us as we explore the art of fermentation and share recipes for homemade fermented sauces, along with creative uses that will elevate your culinary creations.

1. Kimchi

- Description: Kimchi is a traditional Korean fermented vegetable dish, typically made with Napa cabbage, radishes, and spices like garlic, ginger, and chili peppers. It's tangy, spicy, and packed with umami flavor, perfect for adding a punch of flavor to rice bowls, tacos, or stir-fries.
- Creative Use: Use kimchi as a topping for burgers or hot dogs, stir it into fried rice or noodles, or blend it into dressings and sauces for a unique and flavorful twist.

2. Sauerkraut

- Description: Sauerkraut is a fermented cabbage dish that originated in Germany and Eastern Europe. It's tangy, crunchy, and full of probiotics, making it a nutritious addition to sandwiches, salads, or sausage dishes.
- Creative Use: Use sauerkraut as a topping for bratwurst or Reuben sandwiches, mix it into potato salads or coleslaw, or serve it alongside roasted meats or grilled sausages for a tangy and flavorful accompaniment.

3. Hot Sauce

- Description: Hot sauce is a spicy condiment made from chili peppers, vinegar, and salt. It adds heat and flavor to a wide range of dishes, from eggs and tacos to soups and stews.
- Creative Use: Use hot sauce as a marinade for chicken wings or shrimp, mix it into dips or spreads, or drizzle it over pizza, tacos, or grilled vegetables for an extra kick of flavor.

Recipes for Homemade Fermented Sauces

- Homemade Kimchi: Ferment Napa cabbage, radishes, and carrots with garlic, ginger, chili flakes, and fish sauce for a tangy and spicy kimchi that's perfect for adding depth of flavor to Asian-inspired dishes.
- Classic Sauerkraut: Ferment shredded cabbage with salt and caraway seeds until tangy and crunchy for a classic sauerkraut that's perfect for serving with sausages, pork chops, or grilled cheese sandwiches.
- Fiery Fermented Hot Sauce: Ferment a mixture of chili peppers, garlic, onions, and vinegar until bubbly and tangy, then blend until smooth for a homemade hot sauce that's sure to add heat and flavor to any dish.

Creative Uses

- Kimchi Fried Rice: Stir-fry cooked rice with kimchi, scallions, and diced vegetables for a flavorful and satisfying meal that's perfect for using up leftovers.
- Sauerkraut and Apple Salad: Toss shredded sauerkraut with sliced apples, walnuts, and a tangy vinaigrette for a refreshing and crunchy salad that's packed with flavor and nutrition.
- Hot Sauce-Marinated Chicken Wings: Marinate chicken wings in a mixture of hot sauce, soy sauce, and honey before grilling or

baking for spicy and sticky wings that are perfect for game day or backyard BBQs.

With these fermented sauce recipes and creative uses, you can explore the world of fermentation and add depth of flavor and beneficial probiotics to your dishes. Whether you're making homemade kimchi, sauerkraut, or hot sauce, these fermented delights are sure to elevate your culinary creations and delight your taste buds.

Chapter 16: Infused Oils and Vinegars

Elevate your dishes with the exquisite flavors of infused oils and vinegars. In this chapter of "Sauce Secrets: A Restaurant Sauces Cookbook," we delve into the art of infusing olive oils and vinegars with aromatic herbs, spices, fruits, and more, creating a symphony of flavors that will tantalize your taste buds. Join us as we explore techniques for making infused oils and vinegars at home, and discover creative ways to incorporate these culinary treasures into your favorite recipes.

1. Garlic-Infused Olive Oil

- Description: Garlic-infused olive oil adds depth and richness to dishes with its fragrant aroma and subtle garlic flavor. Drizzle it over roasted vegetables, pasta dishes, or grilled meats for a burst of flavor.
- Technique: Heat olive oil gently with peeled garlic cloves until fragrant, then let it cool and strain out the garlic cloves before bottling.

2. Raspberry Balsamic Vinegar

- Description: Raspberry balsamic vinegar balances sweet and tangy flavors, making it the perfect addition to salads, marinades, or fruit desserts. Its vibrant color and fruity aroma add visual appeal to dishes.
- Technique: Combine fresh raspberries with balsamic vinegar in a jar and let them infuse for several days to a week, then strain out the berries before using.

3. Chili Oil

- Description: Chili oil adds a spicy kick to dishes with its bold flavor and intense heat. Drizzle it over noodles, stir-fries, or pizza for an extra burst of flavor and heat.

- Technique: Heat vegetable oil with dried chili flakes, garlic, and ginger until fragrant and infused with flavor, then strain out the solids before bottling.

Techniques for Making Infused Oils and Vinegars at Home

- Choose High-Quality Ingredients: Use fresh, high-quality ingredients for the best results. Opt for extra virgin olive oil for infused oils and aged balsamic vinegar for infused vinegars.
- Experiment with Flavors: Get creative with your flavor combinations by experimenting with different herbs, spices, fruits, and aromatics. Try infusing oils with rosemary, thyme, or citrus zest, or vinegars with strawberries, figs, or herbs.
- Be Patient: Infusing oils and vinegars takes time, so be patient and allow the flavors to develop slowly over several days to a week. Taste periodically and adjust the infusion time to suit your preferences.
- Store Properly: Store infused oils and vinegars in a cool, dark place away from heat and light to preserve their flavors and freshness. Use airtight bottles or jars to prevent oxidation and spoilage.

With these techniques for making infused oils and vinegars at home, you can elevate your dishes with complex flavors and aromas that will impress your family and friends. Whether you're drizzling garlic-infused olive oil over roasted vegetables, raspberry balsamic vinegar over a summer salad, or chili oil over noodles, these infused treasures are sure to take your culinary creations to the next level.

Chapter 17: Quick and Easy Sauces

In the hustle and bustle of daily life, sometimes we need quick and easy solutions to create delicious meals without sacrificing taste or quality. In this chapter of "Sauce Secrets: A Restaurant Sauces Cookbook," we explore a variety of sauces that can be whipped up in minutes, from speedy marinara to blender salsa and stir-fry sauce. These busy weeknight solutions are perfect for those times when you need a flavorful meal in a hurry. Join us as we share shortcut techniques and creative recipes that will help you get dinner on the table in no time.

1. 5-Minute Marinara Sauce

- Description: This quick and easy marinara sauce comes together in just 5 minutes, making it perfect for busy weeknights. Made with canned tomatoes, garlic, olive oil, and Italian herbs, it's a flavorful sauce that's perfect for pasta, pizza, or chicken parmesan.
- Shortcut Technique: Use canned crushed tomatoes and dried herbs to save time without sacrificing flavor. Simmer the sauce for a few minutes to allow the flavors to meld together.

2. Blender Salsa

- Description: This fresh and vibrant salsa is made entirely in the blender, requiring minimal chopping and prep work. Simply blend together tomatoes, onions, jalapenos, cilantro, lime juice, and spices for a delicious salsa that's perfect for dipping or topping tacos, burritos, or grilled fish.
- Shortcut Technique: Use canned diced tomatoes and jarred jalapenos to save time on chopping. Adjust the heat level by adding more or less jalapenos to suit your taste preferences.

3. Stir-Fry Sauce

- Description: This versatile stir-fry sauce is perfect for creating quick and flavorful stir-fry dishes with your favorite proteins and vegetables. Made with soy sauce, garlic, ginger, sesame oil, and a touch of honey or brown sugar, it's a balanced sauce that's perfect for tossing with noodles, rice, or quinoa.
- Shortcut Technique: Use pre-minced garlic and ginger from the grocery store to save time on prep work. Adjust the sweetness and saltiness of the sauce to suit your taste preferences.

Busy Weeknight Solutions for Delicious Meals in a Hurry

- Quick and Easy Pasta Primavera: Toss cooked pasta with 5-minute marinara sauce, sautéed vegetables, and grated Parmesan cheese for a simple and satisfying meal that's ready in minutes.
- Speedy Chicken Fajitas: Sauté sliced chicken breast with bell peppers and onions, then toss with stir-fry sauce and serve in tortillas with blender salsa, guacamole, and sour cream for a quick and flavorful Tex-Mex dinner.
- Weeknight Veggie Stir-Fry: Stir-fry your favorite vegetables with tofu or shrimp, then toss with stir-fry sauce and serve over rice or noodles for a healthy and satisfying meal that's packed with flavor.

With these quick and easy sauce recipes and busy weeknight solutions, you can create delicious meals in a hurry without sacrificing taste or quality. Whether you're craving pasta, tacos, or stir-fry, these shortcut techniques and creative recipes are sure to become staples in your kitchen repertoire. So the next time you're pressed for time, reach for these quick and easy sauces and enjoy a flavorful meal in minutes!

Chapter 18: Exotic Sauces from the Middle East

Embark on a culinary journey through the Middle East with the exotic sauces featured in this chapter of "Sauce Secrets: A Restaurant Sauces Cookbook." From creamy tahini sauce to zesty muhammara and tangy labneh, these rich and flavorful sauces showcase the vibrant flavors of the region, with ingredients like tahini, pomegranate, and sumac taking center stage. Join us as we explore the art of Middle Eastern cuisine and share serving suggestions that pair these sauces perfectly with falafel, kebabs, and mezze spreads.

1. Tahini Sauce

- Description: Creamy and nutty, tahini sauce is made from ground sesame seeds, lemon juice, garlic, and olive oil. It's a versatile condiment that's perfect for drizzling over falafel, kebabs, or grilled vegetables.
- Serving Suggestions: Serve alongside falafel wraps or platters, drizzle over grilled chicken or lamb kebabs, or use as a dip for crudites or pita bread.

2. Muhammara

- Description: Muhammara is a vibrant red pepper and walnut dip flavored with pomegranate molasses, garlic, and spices. It's sweet, spicy, and tangy, with a rich and complex flavor profile that pairs perfectly with grilled meats or spread on flatbread.
- Serving Suggestions: Serve as a dip with pita bread or crudites, spread on sandwiches or wraps, or use as a topping for grilled fish or chicken.

3. Labneh

- Description: Labneh is a tangy and creamy strained yogurt cheese that's similar to Greek yogurt but thicker and more flavorful. It's often seasoned with herbs, spices, or olive oil and served as a dip or spread alongside mezze platters or grilled meats.
- Serving Suggestions: Serve with fresh herbs and olive oil as a dip for vegetables or bread, spread on toast or crackers with honey or jam, or use as a topping for salads or grilled meats.

Serving Suggestions with Falafel, Kebabs, and Mezze Spreads

- Falafel Platter with Tahini Sauce: Serve freshly fried falafel balls on a platter with tahini sauce for dipping, alongside tabbouleh salad, pickled vegetables, and warm pita bread for a satisfying and flavorful meal.
- Grilled Kebabs with Muhammara: Skewer marinated chicken or beef kebabs and grill until cooked through, then serve with muhammara sauce for dipping, alongside rice pilaf, grilled vegetables, and a refreshing cucumber salad for a Middle Eastern-inspired feast.
- Mezze Spread with Labneh: Create a mezze platter with an assortment of dips and spreads, including labneh seasoned with za'atar, hummus, baba ganoush, and olives, served alongside falafel, grilled halloumi cheese, stuffed grape leaves, and warm flatbread for a festive and flavorful spread.

With these exotic sauce recipes and serving suggestions, you can recreate the vibrant flavors of the Middle East in your own kitchen. Whether you're hosting a dinner party or simply craving a taste of the exotic, these rich and flavorful sauces are sure to impress your guests and transport your taste buds to distant lands. So gather your ingredients and get ready to embark on a culinary adventure through the Middle East!

Chapter 19: Chutneys and Relishes

Explore the delightful world of chutneys and relishes with the recipes featured in this chapter of "Sauce Secrets: A Restaurant Sauces Cookbook." From sweet and tangy mango chutney to tart cranberry relish and savory tomato chutney, these versatile condiments are perfect for adding flavor and flair to a wide range of dishes. Join us as we delve into the art of chutney and relish making, and discover pairing ideas that will elevate your meals, from cheeses and grilled meats to sandwiches and beyond.

1. Mango Chutney

- Description: Mango chutney is a sweet and tangy condiment made from ripe mangoes, onions, vinegar, sugar, and spices like ginger, garlic, and chili peppers. It's a versatile accompaniment that pairs well with grilled meats, cheeses, and curries.
- Pairing Ideas: Serve alongside grilled chicken or pork chops, spread on sandwiches or burgers, or serve as a topping for cheese platters or naan bread for a burst of tropical flavor.

2. Cranberry Relish

- Description: Cranberry relish is a tart and tangy condiment made from fresh cranberries, oranges, sugar, and spices like cinnamon and cloves. It's a classic accompaniment to Thanksgiving turkey but also pairs well with cheeses, roasted meats, and sandwiches.
- Pairing Ideas: Serve alongside roast turkey or ham, spread on crostini with goat cheese, or use as a topping for grilled salmon or pork tenderloin for a festive and flavorful touch.

3. Tomato Chutney

- Description: Tomato chutney is a savory and tangy condiment made from ripe tomatoes, onions, vinegar, sugar, and spices like mustard seeds, cumin, and chili peppers. It's a versatile accompaniment that pairs well with cheeses, grilled meats, and sandwiches.
- Pairing Ideas: Serve alongside grilled cheese sandwiches or paninis, spoon over grilled chicken or fish, or serve as a topping for bruschetta or flatbread pizzas for a burst of flavor.

Pairing Ideas with Cheeses, Grilled Meats, and Sandwiches

- Cheese Platter with Assorted Chutneys and Relishes: Create a cheese platter with a variety of cheeses, such as brie, cheddar, and blue cheese, and serve alongside bowls of mango chutney, cranberry relish, and tomato chutney for a flavorful and festive appetizer spread.
- Grilled Meat Sampler with Chutneys and Relishes: Grill a selection of meats, such as chicken, pork, and lamb, and serve alongside bowls of mango chutney, cranberry relish, and tomato chutney for dipping or spreading, along with grilled vegetables and crusty bread for a delicious and satisfying meal.
- Gourmet Sandwich Bar with Chutneys and Relishes: Set up a sandwich bar with an assortment of bread, meats, cheeses, and toppings, including bowls of mango chutney, cranberry relish, and tomato chutney for adding flavor and flair to sandwiches, wraps, or paninis for a customizable and crowd-pleasing lunch or dinner option.

With these chutney and relish recipes and pairing ideas, you can spice up your meals and add a burst of flavor to any dish. Whether you're serving grilled meats, cheeses, or sandwiches, these sweet and savory condiments are sure to impress your guests and elevate your culinary creations. So get ready to explore the delicious world of chutneys and relishes and discover new ways to enhance your favorite foods!

Chapter 20: Gourmet Dipping Sauces

Indulge in the world of gourmet dipping sauces with the tantalizing recipes featured in this chapter of "Sauce Secrets: A Restaurant Sauces Cookbook." From luxurious truffle aioli to zesty cilantro-lime dipping sauce and tangy horseradish cream, these delectable condiments are perfect for elevating appetizers and finger foods to new heights of flavor and sophistication. Join us as we explore the art of gourmet dipping sauces and share recipes that are perfect for entertaining or special occasions.

1. Truffle Aioli

- Description: Truffle aioli is a creamy and indulgent dipping sauce made with mayonnaise, garlic, lemon juice, and truffle oil. It's rich, flavorful, and perfect for dipping fries, roasted vegetables, or seafood.
- Recipe for Entertaining: Truffle Aioli is a perfect accompaniment for a gourmet charcuterie board, offering a luxurious dipping option for meats, cheeses, and crackers.

2. Horseradish Cream

- Description: Horseradish cream is a tangy and spicy dipping sauce made with sour cream, horseradish, Dijon mustard, and lemon juice. It's bold, flavorful, and perfect for serving with roast beef, steak bites, or smoked salmon.
- Recipe for Special Occasions: Horseradish Cream is an ideal pairing for prime rib or beef tenderloin sliders, offering a zesty and refreshing contrast to the rich and savory meat.

3. Cilantro-Lime Dipping Sauce

- Description: Cilantro-lime dipping sauce is a bright and citrusy condiment made with Greek yogurt, cilantro, lime juice, garlic, and jalapeno. It's fresh, vibrant, and perfect for dipping grilled shrimp, chicken skewers, or vegetable crudités.

- Recipe for Entertaining: Cilantro-Lime Dipping Sauce is a refreshing accompaniment for a summer BBQ, offering a burst of flavor to grilled meats and vegetables.

Recipes for Entertaining or Special Occasions

- Gourmet Appetizer Platter: Create a gourmet appetizer platter with an assortment of dips and spreads, including Truffle Aioli, Horseradish Cream, and Cilantro-Lime Dipping Sauce, served alongside an array of crudites, artisan crackers, and cured meats for an elegant and sophisticated appetizer spread.
- Seafood Tower: Serve a seafood tower with an assortment of fresh shellfish, including oysters, shrimp, and crab claws, accompanied by Truffle Aioli, Horseradish Cream, and Cilantro-Lime Dipping Sauce for dipping, along with lemon wedges and cocktail sauce for a luxurious and indulgent dining experience.
- Finger Food Buffet: Set up a finger food buffet with an assortment of bite-sized appetizers, such as chicken skewers, meatballs, and vegetable spring rolls, served with Truffle Aioli, Horseradish Cream, and Cilantro-Lime Dipping Sauce for dipping, along with a selection of dipping bowls and cocktail picks for easy serving and enjoyment.

With these gourmet dipping sauce recipes and serving ideas, you can elevate your appetizers and finger foods to new heights of flavor and sophistication. Whether you're entertaining guests or celebrating a special occasion, these luxurious dipping sauces are sure to impress and delight your guests' taste buds. So get ready to indulge in the delicious world of gourmet dipping sauces and take your culinary creations to the next level!

Chapter 21: Sous Vide Sauces

Welcome to the innovative world of sous vide sauces, where precision cooking meets culinary creativity. In this chapter of "Sauce Secrets: A Restaurant Sauces Cookbook," we explore the art of sous vide techniques for perfectly cooked proteins paired with flavorful sauces. From rich red wine reductions to decadent compound butters and herb-infused oils, these sous vide sauces elevate dishes to new heights of taste and texture. Join us as we delve into the techniques for achieving precise temperatures and textures, ensuring that every bite is a culinary delight.

1. Red Wine Reduction

- Description: A velvety and luxurious sauce, red wine reduction is made by simmering red wine with aromatics and herbs until it thickens into a rich and flavorful sauce. Perfect for drizzling over sous vide steaks, lamb chops, or duck breasts.
- Sous Vide Technique: Sous vide your protein to the desired doneness, then finish by searing in a hot pan. Use the juices and drippings from the sous vide bag to create the base for your red wine reduction, adding depth of flavor and complexity.

2. Compound Butters

- Description: Compound butters are a versatile and decadent addition to sous vide proteins, adding richness and flavor with each bite. Made by mixing softened butter with herbs, spices, and other flavorings, compound butters can be customized to complement a wide range of dishes.
- Sous Vide Technique: Prepare your sous vide protein as usual, then finish by searing in a hot pan. Top the protein with a pat of compound butter just before serving, allowing it to melt and infuse the meat with its delicious flavors.

3. Herb-Infused Oils

- Description: Herb-infused oils add a burst of freshness and aroma to sous vide proteins, enhancing their natural flavors with vibrant herbs and spices. Whether drizzled over fish, chicken, or vegetables, herb-infused oils elevate dishes with their bright and fragrant essence.
- Sous Vide Technique: Infuse your favorite herbs and spices into high-quality olive oil using the sous vide method, allowing the flavors to meld together slowly and evenly. Once infused, use the herb-infused oil to finish off your sous vide dishes, adding a final touch of flavor and elegance.

Tips for Achieving Precise Temperatures and Textures

- Use a Reliable Sous Vide Device: Invest in a high-quality sous vide immersion circulator or water oven to ensure precise temperature control and consistent results with your sous vide cooking.
- Prep Ingredients Properly: Properly season and vacuum-seal your proteins before sous vide cooking to ensure maximum flavor and tenderness. For sauces, use high-quality ingredients and fresh herbs and spices to enhance their flavors.
- Monitor Cooking Times Carefully: Keep an eye on cooking times and temperatures to prevent overcooking or undercooking your proteins. Use a digital thermometer to check internal temperatures and adjust cooking times as needed.
- Experiment and Have Fun: Sous vide cooking is all about experimentation and creativity, so don't be afraid to try new flavor combinations and techniques. Have fun exploring different sauces and pairings to discover your own culinary masterpieces.

With these sous vide sauce recipes and techniques, you can elevate your culinary creations to new heights of flavor and sophistication. Whether you're cooking for a special occasion or simply indulging in a gourmet meal at home, sous vide sauces are sure to impress and delight your taste buds. So fire up your sous vide device and get ready to experience the delicious world of sous vide cooking!

Chapter 22: Holiday and Festive Sauces

Celebrate the joy of the season with the delightful sauces featured in this chapter of "Sauce Secrets: A Restaurant Sauces Cookbook." From tangy cranberry orange sauce to rich gravy with pan drippings and refreshing mint chimichurri, these seasonal sauces are the perfect accompaniment to holiday feasts and celebratory meals. Join us as we explore recipes tailored for Thanksgiving, Christmas, Easter, and other festive occasions, adding a touch of culinary magic to your holiday gatherings.

1. Cranberry Orange Sauce

- Description: Bursting with the flavors of tart cranberries and bright oranges, cranberry orange sauce is a classic accompaniment to Thanksgiving and Christmas dinners. It's sweet, tangy, and perfect for pairing with roast turkey or ham.
- Holiday Pairing: Serve alongside roast turkey or glazed ham, adding a vibrant pop of color and flavor to your holiday table.

2. Gravy with Pan Drippings

- Description: Rich and savory, gravy made with pan drippings is the quintessential sauce for Thanksgiving and Christmas dinners. Made with drippings from roasted meats, flour, broth, and seasonings, it's the perfect finishing touch to your holiday meal.
- Holiday Pairing: Spoon generously over slices of roast turkey, mashed potatoes, and stuffing, creating a comforting and satisfying dish that captures the essence of the season.

3. Mint Chimichurri

- Description: Mint chimichurri is a refreshing and vibrant sauce made with fresh mint, parsley, garlic, olive oil, and vinegar. It's a versatile condiment that adds brightness and flavor to grilled meats, seafood, or roasted vegetables.

- Holiday Pairing: Serve alongside lamb chops or roast leg of lamb for Easter dinner, adding a burst of freshness and herbaceous flavor to the rich and savory meat.

Recipes for Thanksgiving, Christmas, Easter, and Other Festive Occasions

- Thanksgiving Turkey with Cranberry Orange Sauce: Roast a whole turkey until golden brown and juicy, then serve with homemade cranberry orange sauce for a classic Thanksgiving feast that's sure to impress your guests.
- Christmas Ham with Gravy: Glaze a spiral-cut ham with brown sugar and pineapple juice, then roast until caramelized and tender. Serve slices of ham with rich gravy made from the pan drippings for a festive Christmas dinner that will delight your family and friends.
- Easter Lamb with Mint Chimichurri: Grill or roast a rack of lamb until cooked to perfection, then serve with homemade mint chimichurri sauce for a refreshing and flavorful Easter celebration that's sure to become a family favorite.

With these holiday and festive sauce recipes, you can add a touch of seasonal magic to your holiday feasts and celebratory meals. Whether you're hosting Thanksgiving, Christmas, Easter, or another special occasion, these sauces are sure to delight your guests and create lasting memories around the table. So gather your loved ones, raise a toast to the season, and enjoy the delicious flavors of the holidays with these delightful sauces!

❖ Conclusion

As we come to the end of "Sauce Secrets: A Restaurant Sauces Cookbook," it's clear that sauces are the unsung heroes of the culinary world, capable of transforming even the simplest dish into a culinary masterpiece. Throughout this journey, we've explored a vast array of sauces, from classic French reductions to exotic Middle Eastern chutneys, and from quick and easy marinades to luxurious sous vide creations.

The versatility of sauces knows no bounds, as they enhance flavors, add complexity, and elevate the dining experience to new heights. Whether it's a rich gravy accompanying a roast, a zesty salsa brightening up a taco, or a velvety chocolate ganache drizzled over a decadent dessert, sauces have the power to tantalize the taste buds and evoke a symphony of sensations with every bite.

But beyond their culinary prowess, sauces also serve as a canvas for creativity and experimentation. From tweaking ingredients to adjusting seasoning, the art of sauce-making offers endless opportunities for innovation and refinement. So don't be afraid to get adventurous in the kitchen, and let your imagination run wild as you explore new flavor combinations and techniques.

As you continue to hone your sauce-making skills, remember that practice makes perfect, and each batch is an opportunity to learn and grow. Whether you're a seasoned chef or a home cook just starting out, there's always something new to discover in the world of sauces.

We invite you to share your feedback and experiences with the recipes in this cookbook. Whether you've mastered a particular sauce or encountered a challenge along the way, we value your insights and look forward to hearing about your sauce-making adventures. Together, let's continue to celebrate the artistry of sauces and savor the joy they bring to the table.

www.ingramcontent.com/pod-product-compliance
Lightning Source LLC
Chambersburg PA
CBHW051820130726
47987CB00003B/1334